Cambridge University Student Union
International 2003-2004

Cambridge University Student Union International 2003-2004

International Students' Struggle for Representation in the United Kingdom

Christian Kim

The Hermit Kingdom Press
Cheltenham ♦ Seoul ♦ Bangalore ♦ Cebu

**CAMBRIDGE UNIVERSITY STUDENT UNION
INTERNATIONAL 2003-2004:
INTERNATIONAL STUDENTS' STRUGGLE FOR
REPRESENTATION IN THE UNITED KINGDOM**

Copyright © 2005 by Christian Kim

All rights reserved. No part of this book may be reproduced in any form or by any means, electronic or mechanical, including photocopying, recording, or by any information storage and retrieval system, without permission in writing from the publisher.

ISBN 1-59689-043-6 (Hardcover)
ISBN 1-59689-044-4 (Paperback)
ISBN 1-59689-045-2 (Adobe E-Book)

US Library of Congress Control Number: 2005928632

Write-To Address:

The Hermit Kingdom Press
3741 Walnut Street, Suite 407
Philadelphia, PA 19104
United States of America

Info@TheHermitKingdomPress.com

Hermit Kingdom
12 South Bridge, Suite 370
Edinburgh, EH1 1DD
Scotland

http://www.TheHermitKingdomPress.com

In Memory of Pope John Paul II

Contents

Section 1: The Setting - - - - - - - - - - 11

Section 2: The Color Problem - - - - - 23

Section 3: The Visa Problem - - - - - - 51

Section 4: Unity Solution - - - - - - - - - 89

Section 5: My Articles - - - - - - - - - - - 109

"As a dog returns to its vomit,
so a fool repeats his folly."

Proverbs 26:11
The Holy Bible

Section 1: The Setting

CUSU International – or Cambridge University Student Union International – may not be widely known around the world or even in the general setting of the United Kingdom, but it has made a fundamental impact on the British society and compelled key changes in Cambridge University, one of the world's oldest (and some may say, most antiquated) universities in the world.

While there are many great things about Cambridge University – such as a great library and many intellectual thinkers – there are many things that need to be changed. Some of the needed changes for Cambridge University parallel the changing demographics of the British society and the shifting composition of the Cambridge University student body.

Although it is possible that some in the Cambridge University structure resent the infusion of lily-white Cambridge University with students of color, it is a fact and a reality that cannot be ignored. What is needed is structural and thematic change to meet the changing needs of Cambridge University.

Unfortunately, Cambridge University has been too slow in identifying areas of need and change. In fact, Cambridge University today seems bent on denying the cultural and etiquette diversity that pervades the quickly diversifying Cambridge social scene. The definition of politeness shifts with influx of different cultures.

To American and Italian ears, English people speak in a whisper. Americans can be seen as brazen and rude. Italians can be seen as noisy and aggressive. English sensibilities can be ruffled. That may be the cost of diversity and Cambridge University must be prepared to embrace diversity and differences in culture and ways of relating to each other.

There are fundamental changes needed in perception and attitudes. Of course, it is very difficult to change these as many English people, growing up in an homogeneous environment (the United Kingdom is about 92 per cent white) may feel offended by the very differences they encounter and misinterpret differences for something far more negative in their eyes.

While it is very difficult to shift perceptions – particularly among a people who do not want their perceptions modified – it is possible to bring about policy changes that can meet the growing need of the international student community.

Although it is difficult to make people to be open to different cultures and to accept garlic-laden food as good food, it is possible to bring about a structural modification so that those who consume garlic-laden food are represented in a society where garlic-laden food is not much appreciated.

This is where CUSU International comes in. CUSU International exists to represent the needs of international students, who are growing in number.

And international students are different from British students. In some cases, the differences are as great as night and day. Several months ago Oxford University hit news headlines in the United Kingdom. Because of budgetary mismanagement, Oxford University is compelled to accept over 15 per cent more international students into its student body in the next couple of years. Oxford's financial crisis may force a triumph of diversity but it can also sound a social crisis arising from administrative and social mismanagement.

You cannot accept more international students because they pay five times more tuition fees than British students and then ignore their needs. Accepting more international students comes with responsibilities. Charging international students far more money than British students obligates Oxford University (ethically) to meet their needs.

In the same way, Cambridge University is ethically bound to meet the needs of the international student community. Unfortunately, this is not being done. Cambridge University administration has shown no real interest in meeting the needs of international students.

There is practically no support network – emotionally, structurally, information-wise, administratively – for international students at Cambridge University although they pay higher fees than British students. International students are milked for tuition money and then often treated as second-class citizens.

It's not surprising given that many international students actually come from former colonies of England. It is difficult to deny that English history plays a role in the perception of international students. After centuries of colonialism in Asia and Africa, it would be wrong to assume that there are no prejudices against the people of color. But often, this is the assumption that Cambridge University and its officials take and more often than not they make terrible mistakes on account of their presumption.

Given that there are not really any official structures to help the needs of Cambridge University's international students, the responsibility falls on international students themselves. Fortunately for international students, many who came to be involved with CUSU International took their work seriously.

For many officers of CUSU International, they did not see their position as a vainglory position but as a real opportunity to make positive differences in the lives of international students, who lack proper access, adequate representation, and real possibilities for advancement (in many cases).

I have been elected twice to serve as the Academic Officer of CUSU International. My first term was for 2002-2003. I was re-elected for the 2003-2004 term.

While I believe we did a lot of good during the 2002-2003 term, I know that all that we have accomplished during that time pales in comparison to the work of the CUSU International committee that I worked with during 2003-2004. I was the only one who was re-elected, so everybody else was new.

I believe that right people were elected and selected for the positions that they filled. This reality made CUSU International into a force that was feared (and maybe privately hated) in Cambridge University. CUSU International made people look up during the 2003-2004 term and galvanized the international student community in ways that must have frightened some of the Cambridge University administrators who may have preferred that international students remained invisible.

CUSU International had a great team and that made all the difference. These were the officers:

CUSU International Committee Members 2003-2004

(1) Chair: Anna-Mae Koo (Peterhouse)
(2) Secretary: Dheer Mehta (Peterhouse)
(3) Publicity Officer: Mai Yasuhara (Wolfson College)
(4) Academic Officer: Christian Kim (Jesus College)
(5) Welfare Officer: Leah Aw (Emmanuel College)
(6) Freshers' Officer: Shan-Yee Fok (Trinity College)
(7) Social Officer: Earl Deng (Fitzwilliam College)
(8) Colleges Co-ordinator: Andy Pang (Fitzwilliam College)

I don't know if everyone in the committee appreciates all that we were able to accomplish and the lasting historical impact of our labors, but I hope that they can. They have made important contributions for the good of the international student community and the people of color at Cambridge University and they should be proud of what they were able to accomplish.

I do hope that English historians will come to appreciate the extent of positive social impact that we were able to bring about in the Cambridge University context and in the larger context of the British society.

I know that Cambridge University is not quite ready for the deep social changes that are hitting its university. Many people, particularly administrators and staff who have been at Cambridge University for a long time and had seen the recent, sudden influx of the people of color, are deeply resentful although many manage to keep their resentment under wraps, at least publicly.

To give you a picture of the problems facing Cambridge University, I will recount an episode. I published a book on the Korean community, entitled – *Korean-American Experience in the United States: Initial Thoughts*. I went to Queens' College, Cambridge, library to donate my book. The librarian immediately expressed her lack of interest in the book and the reluctance to add the book to Queens' College Library. I asked her if she had any titles on the Korean-American experience. She said no. However, she was still not interested in adding even one book on the topic. She complained about library space. I was disappointed at the attitude. Oxford University quickly added my book to their American Studies library. So at my own university, I would have expected to see a sense of gratitude for wanting to donate a book, particularly on a subject matter for which the library holds no collections. But that was not the case.

This made me realize in a real way that there are people who are not only uninterested in the people of color but also resent the people of color. It may suit their tastes if we continued to remain invisible.

Certainly, there is a lot to be done. CUSU International did as much as we could during our term 2003-2004. We have exceeded our goals in many ways. However, there is still so much to be done.

What we have accomplished is quite encouraging. However, the seeming backlash that seems to be coming is not. I guess it is not surprising in light of the experience of the Civil Rights movement in the United States.

In the United Kingdom, there was never a Civil Rights movement or anything comparable to it. So, in a sense the work we did was the kind of cutting-edge work that Civil Rights leaders engaged in in the past.

The people of color in the United States have many positive leaders who were people of color that they can look back to and learn from in regards to Civil Rights issues. England does not really have any. The people of color who are engaged in trying to empower the people of color on the general level are at the forefront of a cultural revolution.

To be sure, there were individual members of the people of color whom the United Kingdom promoted in the past, even during colonialist days. However, these people of color were often promoted to control the people of color generally and keep the people of color down.

What CUSU International tried to accomplish in 2003-2004 was to benefit all international students and not just a privileged few.

Hopefully, the vision that the committee members of CUSU International 2003-2004 carried with us will spread to our successors at Cambridge University and among the international student population in the United Kingdom.

Section 2: The Color Problem

Cambridge University is a world-class university with many illustrious thinkers who have graced its confines. However, one problem remains large and is gaining confused momentum. Cambridge University has not thought through the question of color and its implications in the quickly changing demographics of the United Kingdom nor even in the more immediate context of Cambridge University. The problem that Cambridge University faces may not be unique to Cambridge University. Symptoms and malaise may be identifiable in other UK institutions. Problems rising from insensitivity to the issue of color or even deliberate brushing aside of a reality that is becoming more poignantly felt does not bode well for the future of Cambridge University.

As many international students are people of color, it is important to ponder questions of access and color as pertaining to Cambridge University and the United Kingdom.

I will first outline problems facing the people of color. In the Cambridge University context, problems can be identified as (1) access, (2) representation, and (3) advancement. I will now elaborate on each of these points.

First, Cambridge University has exhibited its position on the color problem by denying the issue. It is generally perceived in Cambridge that problems facing Cambridge University has to do more with economics and social stratification along financial lines than color. In fact, the issue of color is not raised at all. Most of the access schemes in Cambridge University currently and in past years have shown that economics is the rule by which access schemes are outlined and implemented.

I do not deny the importance of thinking about problems rising from economic stratification in society. It is important to consider financial issues and access issues in terms of economics. However, it is neither accurate in the changing demographics of the United Kingdom nor fair in light of British history to ignore the issue of color.

British society has over 3 million Asians, mostly of Indian, Pakistani, and Chinese descent. In the recent decades, the number of people from the Middle East has been steadily rising. Further adding to the increase in the number of the people of color is the growing influx of people from Africa and the Caribbean. The number of the people of color is increasing so drastically that the current leader of the British Conservative Party, Michael Howard, took out a full-page ad in *The Telegraph* outlining the Conservative Party's desire to protect the British living space and curb immigration. Michael Howard wanted the immigration restriction policy to be the main platform of the Conservative Party as it headed towards British General Elections in May, 2005.

Michael Howard emphasized adopting right-wing border control policy of Australia, for which it has come under serious attack by liberals and moderates in Australia and abroad (and particularly in neighboring Asian countries). Related to this policy is the assault on the asylum system that may actually be in danger of violating the European Union framework laws on the issue. Furthermore, the effort to protect the British *Lebensraum* is implicitly targeting the people of color from India, Pakistan, Africa, and other countries where there are significant numbers of the people of color coming to the United Kingdom.

Certainly, not all British people agree with Michael Howard's aggressive anti-immigration policy. However, for Howard, the leader of one of the two biggest political parties in the United Kingdom, to take out a full-page add in a major British newspaper and make it the British Conservative Party's central platform for the elections at least shows us that the Conservative Party officially believes that such a course of action will win votes. Of course, the result of the elections reals what the British public thinks. Whatever the outcome of the elections, however, it is important to note that Michael Howard and the Conservative Party have taken an aggressive, right-wing stance on immigration. This stems from the visibility of the people of color in the United Kingdom – particularly, those of Asian descent.

The Conservative Party is not alone in desiring less people of color in the United Kingdom. The New Labour has adopted several over-sweeping immigration policies that represent a strong digression from the past.

Anti-immigration policy of Tony Blair is not as aggressively right-wing as Michael Howard's. However, Tony Blair's anti-immigration policy has been seen to be languaged in terms of *Lebensraum* discourse as well. Tony Blair's policies on immigration are directly impacting the Asian community, which has the strongest immigration to the United Kingdom. This is the reason why many in the Asian community have defected to Liberal Democrats, who, at least currently, have a more balanced (Old Labour) approach to immigration.

Certainly, Tony Blair and New Labour recognize the growing number of the people of color and have decided to deal with it by blocking immigration by the people of color. For British New Labour, much energy has been spent on the question of immigration, with many policies adversely affecting the people of color, particularly Asians.

Conversely, Tony Blair's government basically recognizes that there isn't much problem in terms of economic access. And in fact, a person graduating from the University of Essex has just as much chance of making an upper middle class income as someone from Cambridge University. One does not need to come to Cambridge University to make a lot of money or gain important places in society, any more. There is now ready access to wealth in Britain for non-Oxbridge graduates. It may even be possible to say that access to wealth in the United Kingdom is at its easiest in its history.

Further important to note is that one does not necessarily need a university degree to become rich in Britain. Many sports figures make far more money than most Cambridge University graduates can dream of making in the course of their lifetime. Even in non-glamorous jobs, British people are making good living. A person working for public transportation can hope to make about the same as a Cambridge University graduate on the average. Access to wealth in Britain is at its unprecedented high. There is ready economic access, and to a large extent, easy social access as well, for those who may not have much wealth to start.

For Cambridge University to focus on access schemes based primarily on the economic/financial system reflects that Cambridge University administrators and other individuals in leadership do not recognize the present reality of economic mobility and unprecedented open access to wealth. More importantly, in emphasizing access schemes along economic lines, Cambridge University is ignoring an important problem in the British society and at Cambridge University. It is important for Cambridge University to recognize the problem of color, especially in light of current British affairs and the growing tensions in the changing demographics of the United Kingdom.

Besides shifting demographics, there is another reason why Cambridge University must tackle the issue of color. It would be unfair in light of British colonial history, which has continued far into the 20th century, for a major institution of the United Kingdom, like Cambridge University, to ignore the issue of color. Most of the colonized were people of color – particularly, those colonized countries which were most exploited. In other words, there is a clear moral obligation for Cambridge University to consider the question of color seriously.

Despite the compelling reasons from demographics and ethics based on history, Cambridge University has failed to tackle the issue of color. It is high time that Cambridge University changed its wrong course of direction and make things right. In order to do this, it is important to identify the problems.

There are several visible problems relating to the people of color. I will discuss the problems under the heading of (1) access, (2) representation, and (3) advancement.

Access is a big problem for the people of color. It is not easy for the people of color to gain access to Cambridge University. Even when the people of color succeed in gaining access *into* Cambridge University, it is not easy for the people of color to gain access *within* Cambridge University. Thus, the problem of access for the people of color can be viewed on two levels.

I will first discuss the problem of gaining access into Cambridge University. People of color have difficulties gaining access into Cambridge University because of language barriers, cultural differences, and their perception in the British society.

It is understandable why language barriers exist. The people of color often have their native language even when they live in the United Kingdom as British citizens. Thus, it would not be uncommon to find an Indian youth, who is trained in the best schools of the United Kingdom, to have a home setting where an Indian language is spoken. It is possible that the parents of the Indian high school student speak primarily in an Indian language at home. Of course, there can be different degrees of how much Indian language is spoken at home. It is possible to find Indian parents who speak exclusively in an Indian language with their children. Some Indian parents may speak primarily in English with their children, but most will at least use some Indian phrases. We can call the mixture of the two languages, "Englidian." Even for Indians who have lived in the United Kingdom for several generations, Englidian will be spoken to a certain extent.

This is easy to understand. Even if an Indian family is a fourth generation family in the United Kingdom, most likely, they will have Indian relatives in India and Indian relatives in the United Kingdom who are first generation or second generation immigrants.

Many Indians, even those who are born in the United Kingdom, go back to India to find a husband or wife. A part of this reason can be seen as tied to religion. Hindus may want to marry Hindus, and there are more of them in India.

The Indian community is no different from other communities of color. Within the British Asian community, one also finds Chinese individuals who use at least a little Chinese at home. We can call the mixture of Chinese and English as "Chinglish." Even Chinese high school students who are trained at the best boarding schools of the United Kingdom will not be able to escape Chinglish in their home. And like the Indian community, some Chinese people may opt to find a husband or wife in the country of their origin because of their devotion to a Buddhist way of life.

Most communities of color have a completely different language that controls the linguistic reference point or directs linguistic association in the British context.

It is true that some communities of color have English as the primary spoken language. For instance, the Caribbean community, which is rapidly growing in number within the United Kingdom, tends to have English as the primary reference point.

But just because English is spoken in the Caribbean community does not mean that there is not a language barrier between the Caribbean community and the British mainstream society. Just as Englidian and Chinglish – in some cases, primarily English with few foreign words thrown in – can be quite different from the English of the British society, the English spoken by the Caribbean community (which we can call, "Caribbinglish") can be quite different in texture and even content from the English spoken in the mainstream English society.

The fact of the language barrier between Caribbinglish and English should not be difficult to understand. There is a form of language barrier between English spoken in America and English spoken in England. There are expressions in English that do not exist in America. When an English person uses too many of these distinctively English expressions, an American will not be able to understand him even if the language of communication is English. Thus, it is not difficult to understand why Caribbinglish and English are different in important ways.

It is important to recognize that there is a language barrier between the people of color and the British mainstream society. To a certain extent, the language barrier can be seen to be drawn between the British mainstream society English and the language spoken by the communities of color. In a sense, therefore, all the languages spoken by different communities of color in Britain can be seen as belonging to one group.

This grouping is rational from the standpoint of function and result. Functionally, various languages (Englidian, Chinglish, Caribbinglish) act in the same way. They bind communities of color in linguistic distinction from the mainstream British society at large. Sometimes, this is done on a conscious level; at other times, they are done on a subconscious level. Also, in terms of result, different languages of the different communities of color belong together. The result within each community of color is a type of group identity perpetrated by the communal language.

Language barriers that exist between the people of color and the mainstream British society often hurt the access of the people of color in the British society at large. Because of the confines of this study, I will focus on one facet of the British society, the institution of higher education represented in the particular case of Cambridge University. Information provided here will enlighten in the Cambridge University context particularly, but it will also shed light on the dynamics of the British society at large by extension.

How does the language barrier between English and the language of the communities of color hurt the access of the people of color into Cambridge Univresity? The greatest damage is present in the interview process. Just as when one applies for jobs, applications to Cambridge University require interviews. Interviews are an important process to measure the applicant's potential, so there is nothing fundamentally wrong with the interview process. However, given the language barrier, the interview process acts to bar access to the people of color in many instances. In many cases, the denial of access on account of the language barrier is not even recognized.

On this note, it may be appropriate to emphasize that the primary problem in access in this regard stems from the refusal of Cambridge University administrators to recognize the existence of the language barriers. Cambridge University administrators assume that there is only one language operating and it is not only the standard but also the normative. In other words, there is an implicit, subconscious denial of the existence of the language(s) of the people of color.

Applicants who belong to the people of color speak the language of the people of color. As defined earlier, the language of the people of color is a group that is defined against the normative English of the mainstream British society. All languages identified in the group of the people of color share commonality of the grouping against the English of the mainstream in terms of function and result. During the interview process, an applicant who is a person of color will speak from his language reference point.

The interviewer in the Cambridge University context will most undoubtedly not only disregard the existence of the language of the people of color but also penalize the person of color for the language difference. To highlight this point, I will point to Caribbinglish.

Caribbinglish tends to be more expressive and up-front. This is distinguished from the English of the British mainstream which tends to be more subtle and evasive. Whereas some may see this as a difference in style, it is more helpful to see the difference as fundamental. This assertion finds support in the fact that a close study of Caribbinglish and English will exhibit differences in expressions, vocabulary, and sentence structure. Furthermore, associative relationships of language are fundamentally different. A question is raised and a form of answer is expected in the mainstream English language. This is not the same in Caribbinglish. Questions are often raised in different style and format. Answers expected will be different. To answer a Caribbinglish question with an English answer will possibly create misunderstanding. More so the other way around.

Whereas speakers of Caribbinglish are forced to have at least limited dealing with the mainstream English language referent, speakers of mainstream English are not required to (and often do not have opportunities) to come into contact with the Caribbinglish language referent. The problem for the speaker of Caribbinglish is obvious.

The interviewer who holds the key of access to Cambridge University is most likely a speaker with no experience in a Caribbinglish setting. For him, English is normative. Any difference during the interview based purely on the fact and reality of Caribbinglish will not be seen as mere difference but rather as dysfunction, abnormality, violation, and rudeness. It is easy to see the harm that can be directed against the speaker of Caribbinglish even with the best of intents. All people of color experience damage, to a greater or lesser extent, in the current permutation of Cambridge University in the application process. It is easy to see why the people of color's application process will be prejudiced from the very beginning. In other words, the people of color often experience problems of access even before the entry into Cambridge University.

Given the social dynamics, it is not difficult to see why the problem of access exists even after entry into Cambridge University. Cultural differences that exist among (and shared by) the people of color in the society exist in the context of Cambridge University – perhaps, more so because Cambridge University is a controlled setting (at the expense of the people of color). This social reality is patent when we look at social groupings. Often, students of color socialize along color lines. In other words, there is a visible *de facto* segregation (in more cases than not) of the people of color from the general white population. This can be seen in the context of the dining room and bar settings.

When one tries to examine this visible social reality, she is met with difficulties. There are different versions of the story – or different perception of the social reality – based on whom one asks. They generally divide along color lines. If one asks students of color and they answer in an honest way, they are prone to respond by saying that the white student body at large is not welcoming of their presence in the predominantly white group. Some may say that they feel more comfortable within the group of students of color. Often, the "comfort" described is along cultural lines – which include shared food or customs. People of color – whether they are Asians or Afro-Caribbeans – have different foods and customs from the larger white community with shared European-centric traditions and reference points. There are further cultural differences that can be located along the color divide.

When white individuals are asked about the reality of the *de facto* segregation, they often respond in blame of the students of color. It is not uncommon to hear the perception expressed that students of color choose to isolate themselves. Some may say that the students of color are cliquish. Some may even say that they feel that students of color do not like white students. In this, it is possible to detect a mixture of resentment and a feeling of rejection. In other words, some white students believe that students of color choose to group themselves into "a color group" out of their own choice. This differs from the version provided by some students of color that they are "pushed" into the group of students of color by the rejection from white students. Furthermore, because some white students believe that students of color choose to group themselves with students of color, some perceive this as an affront or personal insult. The language sometimes is figured in terms of "they don't like us, so they stick together." A type of us-versus-them dynamics becomes evident.

It is not always easy to determine who is to blame. More likely than not, there is a combination of factors at play. But the fact remains that there is a *de facto* segregation in more cases than not between students of color and white students. Culture plays a role and visible differences may play a role. The fact of the matter is, therefore, many students of color, by definition, do not have access because there is a *de facto* segregation (whatever the reasons may be). The lack of access to larger student body (or the majority) can hurt students of color in different ways.

Perhaps the second major problem may be linked integrally to the first problem. The second problem is representation. Students of color often lack good representation. Given the discussion on access, it is not difficult to see why there would be problem with representtation. If students of color present a visible minority social-reality and are segregated by in large from the majority student body, which tends to be white, then it is not difficult to see why they would not be represented adequately in the context of Cambridge University. It is logical that the majority students will give votes to representatives who they feel represent them. In many cases, this would not be students of color. There is no problem with voting for the candidate of one's choice. That is a democratic prerogative.

The problem, however, is that Cambridge University is a very small community and not really a government. In fact, it is possible to argue that Cambridge University is not really a democratic institution. Cambridge University, like most western universities, can be described as an oligarchy more than anything else. There is a set of rules that are often imposed from top down without any real input from the majority of the university community, which is comprised of students, professors, and staff. In most cases, students comprise the majority of the university community in terms of number but has the least amount of say. This is because the university is arranged in oligarchical terms with power localized among the professors and the administrative body.

However, Cambridge University is a part of the western tradition of universities. And there are many positive ideals tied to the western university tradition. For instance, such ideas as freedom of thought and freedom of expression are cherished in the academic tradition. This value often becomes integrated into the fundamental philosophy of the university. There are other ideals – and some of them tend to be identified with democratic ideals – that become integrally tied to the university – such as student rights and human rights. Professors and university administrators are expected in the western context to make regulations that coincide with the democratic spirit and the tradition of free thinking in the university setting.

Student representation is set up as a way to represent student interests to the university governing body and to help the university administration remember their moral obligetions to the university and the ideals of the western university tradition. In practical terms, however, student representatives have other responsibilities that conflict with their moral obligations to students. In some sense, the student government often plays the role of being intermediary governing bodies for the university.

Unfortunately, student governments are sometimes expected to play the role of a policing body for university policies. Ideally, of course, the student government will put student interests before that of the university administration and university policies. This does not always happen. It is a fact that student governments are becoming increasingly powerful in university settings and play an important role, but they bat for the administration side more so than for the student side. This may be due to the fact that student numbers are increaseing and practical needs of governance demands this channel of control from the perspective of the university administration. Often, university administrators are able to persuade (cajole or coerce) student governments to do their bidding.

Cambridge University is no different. The student government (such as the Cambridge University Student Union) plays a key role in acting as a bridge between the student body and the university administration. Given the large numbers of students, how else would university administers be able to assess the needs and interests than through a student body government that is supposedly voted in by students themselves? Like other universities, Cambridge University student government(s) act(s) as a representative body to the university administration.

It is true that Cambridge University's student government plays the role of representing student interests to the university administration, but Cambridge University's student government also plays the role of relaying Cambridge University interest to students. In other words, Cambridge University student government becomes a part of (or perhaps more accurately, an extended wing of) university administration's effort to govern the student body. In a sense, therefore, Cambridge University student government can share the vested interest of Cambridge University – in whatever form or shape that the vested interest takes. The potential for abuse, therefore, is there.

Given the reality of the function of the student government in the Cambridge University context (as well as any other British university context), it is possible to see why the fact of representation at the student government level can become very important.

Unfortunately, the fact is that students of color often do not participate in any significant way to the direct linking of rule and power. This is truer than not in the Cambridge University context.

It is not surprising to see that students of color who do not normally have significant access in the student body at large (through *de facto* segregation) will have limited (or even adverse) representation at the student government level. This can spell trouble for students of color. We need to remember that the student government at Cambridge University both relays the interests of the students to the university administration and also tries to enforce the interests of the university administration on the student body. There is a two-way representation.

Perhaps, an example will bring out the predicaments of the students of color more poignantly. Let us look at the student governing body, Cambridge University Student Union. Most of the executive officers will be white students from the United Kingdom. The fact that this will normally be the case with any given administration is due to the social dynamics discussed above. There is a type of *de facto* segregation of the students of color, who comprise a small minority of the Cambridge University population. It is logical that the student representative body will have people who identify with the majority.

In the power dynamics that comes to be in this setting, where most of the CUSU execs will be white students, often not very well tuned to the interests of the students of color or the experience of the people of color (due to *de facto* segregation), it would be difficult for CUSU to relay the interests of the students of color to the university administration. There is ignorance to start. Furthermore, when Cambridge University's vested interests conflict with the needs of the students of color, it would be easier than not for CUSU to side with the university administration against the students of color, who represent a minority student body, which is in *de facto* segregation.

It is easy to see why it would be only natural (given the conditions and social dynamics) that the interests of students of color will be bulldozed over in light of the interests that stand against them. This is expected, but it is not necessarily right. In some cases, it would be a morally right thing for the university to consider the needs of the students of color even if it may not be in the visible (or stated) vested interest of the university community at large.

What this means is that the university administration will have to go against what is easy for them to do. It means that the Cambridge University administration will have to consider the needs of the students of color even if that seems like a disadvantage in the short-run.

It is important to state the moral reason why this is important. Cambridge University has a long and illustrated history. For much of the long history of Cambridge University, the student body was basically white. It is only in recent times that the number of students of color has seen a rise. It would not be inaccurate to say that it is only in the last generation – less than 35 years – that there came to be a visible number of students of color. This is certainly different from the British society at large. Although there has been a sharp rise in recent times of the number of the people of color in the United Kingdom, the number of people of color has been gradually increasing for a long time – certainly more than two generations. Thus, the British government has had more time to adapt to changing demographics and the needs of the people of color than the micro-community of Cambridge University.

The sharp rise in number of students of color in recent times has taken Cambridge University by surprise. It is difficult for Cambridge University to cope with the quickly changed social reality and to implement policies to meet the needs of (and protect) the students of color in the new social reality. Given the *de facto* segregation within the student body at large, using the normative channel of student government representation may not suffice to meet the need. There is not adequate representation of student of color through student channels.

Given the explosive social dynamics, Cambridge University is left with a flawed structure. The structure as it exists is not adequate to understand the needs of the students of color and meet the needs of the students of color at large. Student government channels, like CUSU, is flawed, perhaps not by any real fault of their own (given the representative structure), to gauge the needs of the university vis-à-vis students of color.

We see the problems of representation vis-à-vis students of color at Cambridge University and the potential explosion of problems that this will engender for Cambridge Univesity both in the short run and in the long-run.

Problems relating to representation certainly work to impede the advancement of the students of color in Cambridge University. The third problem category of advancement, therefore, can be seen as integrally (and even fundamentally) linked to the problem of representtation. It seems natural to say that without good representation, it is very difficult for the people of color to advance at Cambridge University. Social impediments to adequate representtation will also impede advancement, both directly and in indirect ways.

The problem facing the people of color is an important problem at Cambridge University and is certainly tied to problems facing international students. It would be accurate to say that international students (those students who require a visa to study in the United Kingdom) are predominantly people of color. Thus, problems facing the people of color often find convergence with problems facing international students at Cambridge University.

CUSU International (officially seen as a "campaign" for international students at Cambridge University) has been working hard to bring representation to international students (in indirect – and implicitly direct – ways). But in complete honesty, only the surface has been scratched. This is not to minimize the accomplishments thus far. A lot of hard work has been put in and, perhaps, more than expected (from both sides) have been accomplished. But there is so much more to be done.

In this book, I try to celebrate the important work of CUSU International and give credit where credit is due. However, I am fundamentally a realist (albeit an optimistic one) when it comes to the issue of access for the students of color – who many international students are.

The first step in any lasting solution has to involve in admitting that there is a problem of (1) access, (2) representation, and (3) advancement for the people of color at Cambridge University. Recognizing this problem will be a good constructive step toward solving problems facing the people of color – and by extension, many of the problems facing international students at Cambridge University.

Section 3: The Visa Problem

The biggest struggle to hit the international student community during my term as the academic officer of CUSU International was the imposition of the Visa Renewal Fee by the British New Labour government.

The British New Labour government implemented exorbitant charges in an underhanded way. The whole episode indicated that the British government has not shed itself of its colonialist past or its colonialist government strategies.

The imposition of the Visa Renewal Fee was quickly passed through the British Parliament with hardly anyone noticing. British newspapers did not report about the new legislative changes. Universities did not inform international students about the legislation on the Visa Renewal Fee. This was certainly the case with Cambridge University. Cambridge University administration was completely silent on the matter. Even several months after the Visa Renewal Fee was legally in force, Cambridge University administration refused to inform international students adequately about the matter.

The negligence of Cambridge University vis-à-vis the international students in a matter that is of the greatest impact (as their relationship to the United Kingdom was concerned) is a picture into the general neglect of international students by Cambridge University. At Cambridge University, international students are invisible, by in large, and it seems that Cambridge University wants to keep it that way.

Further difficulty facing international students is the fact that many of the CUSU executive committee members belong to the Labour Party and have aspirations to enter British politics through the Labour Party. (In British politics, it is impossible to enter politics without party support as British politics is Parliamentary in structure, scope, and philosophy.) Many CUSU executive members were not really supportive of the struggle of the international student community at Cambridge University against the new Visa Renewal Fee. This definitely added more difficulties in the struggle of the international students for representation.

To bring the whole matter into focus, let's see what the British New Labour government did. The British New Labour government legislated to raise the Visa Renewal Fee to £250 for the walk-in service (£155 for mail-in service that takes up to 8 weeks or more for processing). Hardly anyone outside of the government was aware that this legislation had gone through. Cambridge University administration, which should have felt obligated to inform its international students, did not.

The British New Labour government made the public announcement on July 10, 2003, about the new Visa Renewal Fee to go into effect on August 1, 2003. Thus, British New Labour government did not even give one month's notice regarding the exorbitant new charge.

It is important to note that Visa Renewal Fee was free before this legislation. To put it into perspective, let's note that the exchange rate is close to 2:1 meaning that two USA dollar is equivalent to one British pound. Thus, the walk-in service was raised from zero to $500. The amount is exorbitant and unfair. It is the equivalent to one month rent.

And let's not forget that this amount is worth one year of college graduate wage in some countries, like India, China, and Indonesia. Students already holding scholarships (when the Visa Renewal Fee was zero) would not have any way of paying the new exorbitant fee. The policy can force bright students from abroad to leave the United Kingdom because they wouldn't be able to afford the exorbitant Visa Renewal Fee.

Just like the Visa Renewal Fee took international students all over the United Kingdom by surprise, it took months for scholarship agencies abroad to find out about it (after government implementation!). Cambridge University administration did not inform its own international students who are directly affected, so it stands to reason that they did not go out of their way to inform any scholarship agencies (especially in other countries) who would need to know to add to the scholarship fund of international students who hold their scholarships in order for them to receive a student visa renewal.. $500 is a lot of money in many Third World countries, which send their brightest to receive degrees in the United Kingdom.

To make matters worse, the British New Labour government made the changes to go into effect on August 1, 2003, during the height of summer (and made their first public announcement in the summer on July 10, 2003). Most of the international students were back in their home countries for the summer vacation.

International students were physically removed from the United Kingdom so it was quite impossible for them to organize a protest. By the time that most international students came back to the United Kingdom, the Visa Renewal Fee would have been in effect for two months. Cambridge University's fall term (Michaelmas Term) started on October 7, 2003.

In fact, out of all the officers of CUSU International, I was the only one in the United Kingdom at the time that the Visa Renewal Fee went into effect. As such, it was up to me to offer the first stage of resistance.

I contacted Anna-Mae Koo, the Chair of CUSU International, in Hong Kong, her native country, then in Japan, where she was doing some internship work during the summertime. Anna-Mae, being a law student at Cambridge University, was aware of the importance of taking the challenge at legal levels and had many great ideas. Unfortunately, some of her ideas could not be implemented with most of the CUSU International officers back in their home countries.

The Welfare Officer, Leah Aw, was back in her native country of Singapore. There was little that she could do from Singapore. Since the whole Visa Renewal Fee hit all of us by surprise, we had no way to prepare for it before most of the CUSU International officers left for their home countries for the duration of the summer.

The whole manner by which the Visa Renewal Fee was implemented by the British New Labour government was underhanded and was the kind of thing that the United Kingdom did during its colonialist days. Any possible representation was minimized before the taxation was put into place. I felt like shouting, "No taxation without representation!"

I myself was only made aware of the new Visa Renewal Fee two weeks before the fee went into effect. It was decided that I should work with Ben Brendid, the president of the CUSU executive committee, and Sarah Airey, the president of the Graduate Union, regarding the Visa Renewal Fee.

I found Ben Brendid, who is a British national, being cautiously supportive of taking up challenges on the matter of the Visa Renewal Fee. Ben correctly understood the implications of the struggle, and I felt that he was a bit worried about being entangled in the struggles of international students against the British government. It is not dissimilar to the reluctance of many Americans to support the Civil Rights movement in the USA against government authorities.

Sarah Airey, who is from West Virginia, was also not very enthusiastic about the struggle. Sarah held a Marshall Scholarship which paid her generously. In fact, the scholarship is one of the best paid scholarships in Cambridge University, so she was not worried about financial matters. $500 probably did not seem like much to her. Furthermore, Sarah did not have to renew her student visa, so it was not really a problem that she personally faced.

There were some student government officials who opposed fighting the Visa Renewal Fee. David Riley, a Graduate Union executive member, said that the British New Labour should be able to charge for the cost of visa renewal. I told him that it does not cost $500 to renew one visa. It's one thing to raise the Visa Renewal Fee from zero to $30, it's a completely different thing to raise the Visa Renewal Fee to $500.

There were clearly challenges within the student government in organizing a fight against the Visa Renewal Fee. As the student officials that I was working with at Cambridge University at that time in the summer were white, I tried to describe the conditions of the Third World and the difficulty for the people of color, many of whom come from countries where $500 can feed a family of four for several months. I was disappointed to see that some did not like my using the term "the people of color" at all. I am not sure what motivated their refusal to acknowledge the people of color and the struggles of the people of color.

Given that there were only two weeks before the Visa Renewal Fee went into effect, we had to focus on constructing a positive battle and that's where I tried to put my focus. Anna Mae Koo, the CUSU International Chair, and Leah Aw, the CUSU International Welfare Officer, tried to do what they could from their home by encouraging CUSU executive members to prioritize the battle against the Visa Renewal Fee.

I don't doubt that some (or even many) in the student government thought that the Visa Renewal Fee was a good idea, like David Riley, but fortunately many went along with our efforts to mount a fight against the British government on the new, exorbitant Visa Renewal Fee. Supporting charging such an exorbitant fee for international students openly would not have been politically correct. I am sure that I made some enemies by prodding and mounting arguments to fight the Visa Renewal Fee. Given that there was only two weeks' time, I pressed the urgency, frequently and strongly.

What made the matter worse is the fact that Cambridge University was not taking the most positive attitude towards the struggle. Since Cambridge University did not inform international students about the Visa Renewal

Fee; they must have felt some guilt. Perhaps, they did not feel guilty at all but were supportive of the Visa Renewal Fee. We cannot rule out that possibility. Particularly since Cambridge University is in essence a state institution, it has a vested interest in supporting the decisions of the state.

After much wrangling and discussion, we decided to produce an open letter. Both Sarah Airey, the Graduate Union president, and Ben Brendid, the CUSU president, were not eager to have me actively participate in the open letter writing process. They were supposed to send me copies of every draft, but both failed to do that with a couple of drafts. It seemed more intentional than not as when I asked Sarah Airey about the copy of the letter, she responded angrily rather than giving me a draft. I was more interested in getting real help for international students, so I tried to work through the complicated mess.

I had to play hardball in order to get them to include all the important factors that they did not agree with. Thankfully, most of the important points were implemented. The cost of my hardball-playing was that they were reluctant to include my name with the open letter. I agreed to go along with signing just the name of Anna-Mae Koo, CUSU International Chair. In hindsight, perhaps, I should have fought to include the name of Leah Aw, CUSU International Welfare Officer, and myself, who did most of the work in person on behalf of

CUSU International when other officers were away in their home countries. But the open letter was already one week late as it was, so there was no time for negotiating fine details. It was important to get help for international students.

Credit should be given to Ben Brendid and Sarah Airey on one point. Although they were not able to get key university administrators (such as the Vice Chancellor) to sign their name on the letter, they were able to get some representatives. Of course, in hindsight, it may have hurt us more than help us to get anyone less than the Vice Chancellor (who is the administrative head of the university, like a university president in the USA; the Chancellor is a figurehead and is Prince Philip, the Duke of Edinburgh) of the university to sign the letter with us because lack of endorsement at the highest administrative levels can be seen as an adverse endorsement by the British Labour government. But at the time, we did not have time to think about these matters or discuss them.

This is the open letter that was sent out a week after the start of the Visa Renewal Fee:

```
The Rt Hon. David Blunkett MP
Secretary of State
The Home Office
50 Queen Anne's Gate
London SW1H 9AT
```

8 August 2003

Dear Secretary of State,

We are writing from the University of Cambridge, with regard to the introduction by the Home Office of charges for the extension of visas. We have several serious concerns about the matter when applied to international students in the UK.

Level of charging

- We have concerns regarding the level of charging involved. The extension fee of £155 is a significant sum. We are especially concerned that the 'premium' service charge of £250 is likely to be incurred by many international students, who may wish to travel with their passports in considerably less time than the maximum of 13 weeks that the process could take. We firmly believe that both charges are an unfair burden on international students.

- Students pursuing research at British universities are particularly likely to be affected by these charges because of the relative unpredictability of final submission dates and oral examinations. It is in the normal course of things for students to need to seek short extensions of perhaps two or three months beyond the original completion date.

Timing of the decision

• There appears to have been little or no consultation with the HE sector on this issue.

• Announcing the policy in mid-July, at a time when most students are not in residence, is unfair. Putting the policy into effect on August 1st 2003 gives universities and student unions very little time to prepare advice, and students themselves even less time to prepare their applications to avoid the charge. It also seems unfair that as most students' visas take effect from mid- to late-September (i.e. just before the start of term), renewal would only be possible after the August 1st charging deadline. For these students, the introduction of the charge takes place effectively without any warning: the full costs of staying in the UK could not have been known to them before they arrived.

Effects of the policy

• We additionally believe that this policy is inconsistent with the Prime Minister's Initiative to encourage international applications to UK Higher Education. Charging for visa extensions and the method by which this policy has been implemented can only serve to tarnish the international image of advanced study in this country.

We conclude that such high charges and the chosen method of their implementation can be seen as exploitation of international students. People who wish to come to this country to study should not be subjected to this additional levy. It is estimated that around 200 international students apply for visa extensions every day, and will therefore find themselves incurring these charges. We therefore urge the Home Office to exempt international students from these charges as soon as possible.

Yours sincerely,

Ben Brinded & Stuart Basten
Cambridge University Students' Union

Dr Penelope Wilson & Mr Ray Jobling
on behalf of the Cambridge Colleges

Matthew Moss
International Education Officer
University of Cambridge

Dr Laurie Friday
Board of Graduate Studies
University of Cambridge

Anna-Mae Koo
Cambridge University Students' Union
International Campaign

CUSU INTERNATIONAL 2003 - 2004

Sarah Airey
Cambridge University Graduate Union

Any reply should be sent to:

Mr Ben Brinded
Cambridge University Students' Union
11/12 Trumpington Street
Cambridge
CB2 1QA

Copies of this letter have been sent to:

The Prime Minister
10 Downing Street
London
SW1A 2AA

Rt Hon Charles Clarke MP
Secretary of State for Education & Skills
Department for Education & Skills
Sanctuary Buildings
Great Smith Street
London
SW1P 3BT

Mr Alan Johnson MP
Minister of State for Higher Education & Lifelong Learning
Department for Education and Skills
Sanctuary Buildings
Great Smith Street
London
SW1P 3BT

Ms Beverley Hughes MP
Minister of State for Citizenship,
Immigration & Counter-Terrorism
The Home Office
50 Queen Anne's Gate
London SW1H 9AT

Mrs Anne Campbell MP
Member of Parliament for Cambridge
House of Commons
SW1A 0AA

Mr Andrew Lansley MP
Member of Parliament for
Cambridgeshire South
House of Commons
SW1A 0AA

Mr Barry Sheerman MP
Chairman of the Education & Skills
Committee
House of Commons
SW1A 0AA

Mr John Denham MP
Chairman of the Home Affairs Select
Committee
House of Commons
SW1A 0AA

Mr Bill Jeffrey
Director General
Immigration & Nationality Directorate
Lunar House
40, Wellesley Road
Croydon
CR9 2BY

Universities UK

CUSU INTERNATIONAL 2003 - 2004

Woburn House
20 Tavistock Square
London
WC1H 9HQ

UKCOSA

The Council for International
Education
9-17 St Albans Place
London
N1 0NX

Times Higher Education Supplement
Admiral House
66-68 East Smithfield
London
E1W 1BX

The Times
1 Pennington Street
London
E98 1TA

The Financial Times
1 Southwark Bridge
London
SE1 9HL

The Guardian
119 Farringdon Road
London
EC1R 3ER

The Independent
Independent House
191 Marsh Wall
London
E14 9RS

I and other officers of CUSU International were sincerely hoping for a reply back. I guess it was more hope than a realistic expectation. The fact is that Cambridge University did not inform its international students about the burdensome Visa Renewal Fee hike. That should say something about what was going on. The fact is that the charge went from zero to $500 and it was done as if done in secret. We were only made aware of the issue a few weeks before the policy came into effect.

And it is important not to forget that British New Labour government was implementing anti-immigration policies, stealthily. Visa Renewal Fee was a part of that as it, in effect, targeted the people of color from poor Third World countries.

I was convinced that this was the first step toward adverse domino effect against international students. If they can increase the Visa Renewal Fee from zero to $500 without any resistance, what is to stop them from raising it another $500 after a few years? Perhaps, I should have kept my thoughts to myself, but as usual, I did not think about protecting myself. I was more interested in the greater benefit to the people of color and in help for all international students, and if it meant I had to stick my head out to be chopped, so be it!

As expected, unfortunately, we received no responses. The British government did not even acknowledge our letter. British newspapers refused to carry this important story or print the open letter. It felt like British newspapers were not interested in reporting the biggest crisis to come to international students in this century but rather interested in protecting the British government and its anti-immigration stance. Granted, we did not send the open letter to all the newspapers in the United Kingdom, but those that received the open letter were not interested in it.

Sarah Airey, the Graduate Union president, and Ben Brendid, the CUSU president, lost interest on the Visa Renewal Fee issue. When I tried to prod them further, they responded by saying that they did all they could. They sent out the open letter.

Of course, there was more to be done, but they did not seem interested. As I had pushed to get them to prioritize the Visa Renewal Issue for a few intense weeks, I thought I had to ease up on them. Anna-Mae Koo, the CUSU International Chair, and Leah Aw, the CUSU International Welfare Officer, and I decided that we should wait for the response in the meanwhile and then regroup in September when all the CUSU International officers would be returning from their home countries back to Cambridge and then organize a challenge to the British government.

When all the other CUSU International officers arrived in Cambridge in September, we still had not received any responses to our open letter. The officers of CUSU International realized that it was all up to us to wage a just war on the British government.

Anna-Mae Koo, the CUSU International Chair, proved to be wise in getting Ben Brendid at least nominally on board to fight the Visa Renewal Fee. As Ben Brendid was the president of CUSU, this lent official respectability to the struggle. In truth, Ben Brendid did not do much, but I don't suppose that his active support was what Anna-Mae was going for. Even if she wanted an active support, she probably would not have received it. But it was enough to get Ben's tacit support. This gave us the opportunity to wage the battle against Visa Renewal Fee at the university-wide level with the official blessing of CUSU. Of course, we had to do all the work and we realized what we were up against.

CUSU International formed a Welfare Committee to focus on the Visa Renewal Fee struggles. Ben Brendid's name was signed on and Leah Aw, as the CUSU International Welfare Officer, became the head of the CUSU International Welfare Committee. Anna-Mae Koo (the CUSU International Chair), Shan-Yee Fok (Freshers' Officer) and I (Academic Officer) became core members of the newly formed committee. We actively recruited volunteers to help.

We identified several key areas of work: (1) petition-signing, (2) organizing universities, (3) lobbying government officials.

CUSU International Welfare Committee felt that organizing petition-signing was a good way to raise awareness of the plight of the international students at Cambridge University. British students can be enlightened about what the Visa Renewal Fee means and how international students are being treated under the British New Labour government. Furthermore, petitions have a real objective as well. We can send in the petitions signed by individuals to government officials and the British government. Here is the petition form designed by Leah Aw, the CUSU International Welfare Officer and the head of the CUSU International Welfare Committee:

STOP INTERNATIONAL VISA RENEWAL CHARGES!

The UK Home Office has recently proposed visa renewal charges of up to £250, which will affect all international students applying for visa renewals after August 1, 2003. CUSU International and CUSU view these charges as completely unjustified for international students, considering the exorbitant fees international students already pay, so it is our goal to reverse this proposal. As part of CUSU International's anti-visa renewal charges campaign, we are holding a university-wide petition, so please take a few seconds to sign this petition. CUSU International also plans to hold debates and discussions with MP's regarding this issue, and we need all the help we can get to stop these charges. More information on this campaign and how to get involved can be found at: www.cusu.cam.ac.uk/representation/international

Name (college)	Country of Origin	E-mail Address

CUSU Internatioanl Welfare Committee members took the petition to their colleges and their departments/faculties. We tried to get as many signatures as possible.

I tried to get signatures at the Faculty of Divinity and Jesus College, Cambridge. As I was doing some research into English Contract Law, English Land Law, and English Equities Law for research into comparative law (with Jewish Law), I was able to get signatures of many law students. In particular, many of the third-year law students at Queens' College, Cambridge, during the 2003-2004 signed the petition in support. But I found that not all students were supportive. Several white students told me to my face that the new, exorbitant Visa Renewal Fee was good. I suspected some white students did not like the increase in the number of the students of color who are visible in their faculty. By in large, however, many were polite about it.

Leah Aw, the CUSU International Welfare Officer, was particularly good about pushing all of us to be aggressive in getting signatures for the petition. Leah actually had the most number of signatures, so she was more hard on herself than she was on others on the committee.

Besides petition drives, CUSU International Welfare Committee tried to organize British universities. The idea was that if we worked together, it would be easier to get the government to overturn the Visa Renewal Fee or minimize it to a more manageable and reasonable levels.

We tried to organize British universities through their student governments. This proved to be more difficult than we had thought. Many British universities did not even have a student government officers dedicated to the needs of international students. Many universities did not even have an official officer in the whole university administration to deal with international students, so it should not be surprising on one level. Even at Cambridge University, a particular office to deal with international students was formed after the Visa Renewal Fee fiasco.

British universities were divided among the CUSU International committee members to contact. Our job was to see if there was an international students' officer at the student government and to see if they were fighting the Visa Renewal Fee.

I was to contact two universities: University of Edinburgh and King's College, London. I was happy to see that the University of Edinburgh was engaged in a form of protest against the Visa Renewal Fee. Although their protest was not as developed as ours, it was good to see that they had one going. In contrast, we found that none of the other British universities were engaged in protesting the Visa Renewal Fee hike. Furthermore and further disturbing was the fact that many student governments were not aware of the new Visa Renewal Fee at the beginning of October, 2003, two months after the Visa Renewal Fee of $500 dollars went into effect.

This disturbing case was the scenario at King's College, London, which is located at the heart of London in the Westside, which is famous for the London theatre scene. King's College, London, has many international students, more so than most other British universities. And King's College, London, is practically a stone's throw from the British seat of government, the Parliament.

I went to King's College, London, and received a hostile reception. It is not surprising since all the student government officials were white and there was not one international student or student of color on full staff at the time. It may be due in part to the fact that the executive members of King's College, London, Student Union were not even aware of the Visa Renewal Fee hike that went into effect two months ago. They were embarrassed about their ignorance, but instead of taking a constructive attitude to work to combat the Visa Renewal Fee hike, some of the members of the King's College, London, took their guilt out on me for being the bearer of news. I was quite disappointed.

Thankfully, a combination of pressure, their dedication to political correctness, and publicly declared allegiance to access issues forced them to pay greater attention to the plight of international students rising from the Visa Renewal Fee. Soon, they appointed a part-time officer to represent international students at King's College, London's Student Union and even participated in trying to get Visa Renewal petitions signed. Several of King's College, London's student government officers did remain somewhat bitter about being compelled to take up the Visa Renewal Fee issue. It may be due to the fact that most student government officers across the United Kingdom tend to be loyal to the British New Labour Party and have political aspirations in the party after their graduation – which for some of them is less than one year away.

Leah Aw, the CUSU International Welfare Officer, tried hard to organize British universities to meet together to discuss the issue, but the meeting did not materialize until over 6 months after we first started to contact other universities. In the meanwhile, we tried to work with individual universities and their representatives on a one-to-one basis. By in large, however, we found our efforts in this regard futile. Many British universities did not have an international students' representative on the student government level or on the university administration level.

In hindsight, we can say that our efforts in this regard were not completely fruitless. Although we could not get British universities adequately organized to combat the Visa Renewal Fee issue, we did raise the awareness of the plight of international students across the United Kingdom. As the result of our contacts, many British universities were compelled to appoint international students' representatives. Student Unions in various British universities were forced, in effect, to create a position for a person to represent international students at their universities on the official student government level.

The National Union of Students, which is the umbrella student government organization that oversees individual university student governments recently created a part-time representative for international students. Although it is a part-time position and does not have much power or say within the National Union of Students structure, it is a step in the right direction. This step in the right direction can be credited to the aggressive efforts in the area of the Visa Renwal Fee campaign by CUSU International. Thus, even if we did not actually succeed in organizing British universities to fight the Visa Renewal Fee, we became an important impetus for British university reform in the area of international students' representation. Hopefully, the positive changes will continue.

Like organizing British universities against the Visa Renewal Fee, contacting British government officials regarding the Visa Renewal Fee was a failure on the intended level of combating the Visa Renewal Fee but a success from the perspective of long-term good for international students.

We knew we were fighting a losing battle but that did not deter us from fighting hard. One way we tried to lobby British government officials was by encouraging British students to contact their MP (what is equivalent in the US to a Senator or a Representative).

We mailed out this letter to interested British students:

```
Cambridge University Student Union
(CUSU) International
11/12 Trumpington Street
Cambridge
CB2 1QA


Dear Socially Conscientious Student at
Cambridge,


Thank you for your interest in lending
support to international students at
Cambridge University by getting
involved and writing a letter to your
MP.

Included is a stamped, addressed
envelop with a letter.  Please sign
the letter and mail it out to your MP.

Thank you for being socially
conscientious and being proactive on
behalf of those who are socially
disadvantaged by the new legislation.
```

CUSU INTERNATIONAL 2003 - 2004

Sincerely,
Christian Kim
CUSU International Welfare Committee
2003-2004

We sent the above letter to British students who expressed interest in joining our fight against the Visa Renewal Fee hike. We included a drafted letter they could send to their MP (Member of the Parliament). Here it is:

Mr. Richard Bacon, MP
South Norfolk Conservative Association
Grasmere
Denmark Street
Diss
Norfolk
IP22 4LE

7 March 2004

Dear Mr. Bacon,

RE: OPPOSITION TO THE VISA RENEWAL CHARGES

I am writing to you to express my utmost concern regarding the new implementation of visa renewal charges pursuant to Immigration and Asylum Act 1999. These charges pose a serious financial burden to international students coming to study in the UK and is a serious violation of the Prime Minister, Tony Blair's stated goal of attracting more international students. (18th June 1999)

Under the Home Office's new policy, international students from outside the European Economic Area (EEA) would have to pay £155 for a postal application (which may take up to 13 weeks to process). The premium same-day service for personal callers costs £250. This cost is incurred each time an application is made. A charge of £36 was also introduced for an initial student visa (for first-time student visa applications).

I am currently a student at the University of Cambridge. International students here are a vital part of the student community contributing to the social, academic and cultural diversity of the university. I have no doubt that this is the case in other universities across the UK.

I do not believe that the implementation of a visa renewal charge is itself unjustified. However, I strongly disagree with the following:

1) The charges were arbitrarily determined and are too high.

In 1999, when the passage of the Immigration and Asylum Act established the principle of visa charging, the then Home Office Minister gave specific and categorical assurances to those in higher and further education that international students would be given special consideration. The estimated charge at the time was given to be £90, significantly lower than the £150 or £250 charged now. As CISUK has pointed out rather pertinently, inflation over the last four years has certainly not been to the tune of 72%. Also special consideration has certainly not been given to international students. The 'negative resolution procedure' was adopted by the government, so that the consultation was only internal and none of the Students' Unions nationwide have been consulted. The second round of consultation promised by the government has not happened either; our Students' Union has tried to contact Beverly Hughes MP with no avail.

2) Application procedure is too lengthy and inefficient.
The application procedure can take up to 13 weeks. 13 weeks is wholly unreasonable already for students to be without their passports. This is compounded by the fact that the academic term here at the University of Cambridge is only 8 weeks long. Students are made to stay in Cambridge to wait for their passport! This is clearly contrary to the stated raison d'etre of the charges—to improve the efficiency of service. In addition, international students have

encountered major problems with the service including cases of lost passports.

I am aware that there is an Early Day Motion 1729 tabled by John Barrett MP expressing my exact concerns. I believe this is a first step to counter these charges.

As a voting constituent, I strongly urge that you take action, starting with signing on to the Early Day Motion. I would appreciate a reply from your Office in response to the issues that I've raised, outlining your stance as well as any further action.

Yours sincerely,

[Student's Name and Address]

Besides encouraging individual Cambridge University students to write to their MPs, the CUSU International Welfare Committee actively encouraged leaders of student groups at Cambridge University to write letters to British government officials. A sample of the letter we encouraged them to write is included below:

CUSU INTERNATIONAL 2003 - 2004

ADDRESS HERE:

.... /.... /2003

Dear Sir/Madam,

RE: Home Office Visa Renewal Charges for International Students

I am writing to you to raise my concern about recent charges to foreign nationals introduced by the Home Office. The attached document gives you background information on these charges and how they may impact on international students already studying or considering studying in the UK. It also includes Cambridge University's official stand, and action undertaken thus far, regarding this issue.

I am the President of
_____ and am writing on behalf of my ____ members.
I am concerned that my members may be financially disadvantaged to the significant tune of
£_____ - this is because, considering the length of Cambridge terms (8weeks) and the extended amount of time needed to

process the visa application (up to 13weeks), most of my members will be compelled to opt for the Premium Service, which costs £250. Additionally, paying that amount does not guarantee a visa permit that lasts till the end of their period of study in the UK – it all depends on the discretion of the reviewer.

I would like to request that these unreasonable charges be revoked, or lowered significantly, and also for an explanation for why they have been imposed in the first place.

These charges have not only affected my existing members adversely – they will undoubtedly also have a deleterious effect on future students from my country who are considering pursuing higher education in the UK.

I hope that you will consider these issues when reviewing the policy.

Thank you for your kind attention!

Yours Sincerely

Our efforts to win Members of Parliament (MPs) to our cause of fighting the Visa Renewal Fee did not succeed ultimately. However, our efforts did not go to waste. Whereas previously, many British MPs did not think about international students and our needs, they were at least forced to think about our side.

And I see our efforts as a success in the long-run because members of the British government were made aware that there is an active international student population that will not take unfair policies lying down. Certainly, this would minimize gratuitous abuse in the future.

Furthermore, there must be well-meaning government officials in the British government, who became more aware of the problems facing international students as the result of our efforts. We can only hope that these conscientious individuals will be encouraged to speak on behalf of international students when unjust policies are in motion against international students.

Of course, it is difficult to gauge the positive impact on the British government as the result of our lobbying efforts – particularly in letter writing. But I guess time will tell the positive impact.

Of course, in the short-run, CUSU International Welfare Committee can be seen to have failed in the Visa Renewal Fee hike crisis. We were not able to force the British government to annul the charges or even mitigate the charges. But certainly our hard efforts paid off in other ways. International students became more "visible" and those in the larger, mainstream British society are learning that they cannot go ignoring the rights and the needs of international students. They realize that any decisions against international students will result in some resistance, however feeble they may seem it to be. This is certainly a step in the right direction.

It is always difficult to take the first step. CUSU International has taken an important first step in the politics of the United Kingdom and in the British university scene to compelling the voices of international students to be heard. And in this regard, CUSU International has made history with real lasting impact.

Section 4: Unity Solution

Certainly, there were many factors that CUSU International faced right from the start, from the beginning of the 2003-2004 period, which is from 2003 Easter Term (April 22-June 13, 2003) to 2004 Lent Term (January 13-March 12, 2004). Within the Cambridge University, there was not a completed structure to deal with international students. Some colleges in the Cambridge University system did not have any student representatives to deal with international student issues. Other colleges had an international officer but not an adequate system to meet the needs of the international students' representative. In short, Cambridge University lacked any real extensive support system for all of its international students.

It is important to note – for the sake of outsiders who are not familiar with the Cambridge University system – that Cambridge University is arranged according to colleges. Each student belongs to a college and is a part of the department/faculty where he or she studies. Thus, if Susan Smith is an English major, she will be a part of the English faculty. However, she will also have a college association. Let's say that Susan is a part of Clare College. Susan, then, will be housed in Clare College's dormitory and will eat normally at Clare College's dining room.

Each college has its own dining room and student government structure. College student government's relationship to the university-wide Cambridge University student government can be compared to a state government in the USA context (in its relationship to the US federal government). There is a university-wide student governing body and that is the Cambridge University Student Union (CUSU). Each college sends representatives (president, vice president, or any other of the college executive officer) to CUSU Council meeting which meets on a regular basis throughout the academic term. Thus, CUSU officers can be seen as a type of executive governing body for the whole university.

It was only in the last couple of years that CUSU International has expanded into a full-blown committee (or "campaign" as CUSU likes to call CUSU International). Even a few years ago, there was no real representation for international students in the expanded CUSU structure. Given that the development within CUSU itself is recent, it is not surprising that many colleges still do not have international students' representatives within their own governing structures. As many students socialize and live within the college structure, the lack of adequate representation for international students can be quite debilitating for some international students. Often, international students seek social outlet in an ethnic student group and become segregated away from the college structure, by in large.

Given the reality of problems facing international students at Cambridge University, CUSU International sought to go to the heart of the problem. We felt that issues of access and representation must be resolved first and foremost. Thus, in a sense, we sought to bring a unity of structure that includes the interests of international students within the structure – there is really one governing structure with CUSU at the center, linked by college student unions.

Andy Pang, CUSU International Colleges Co-ordinator

Andy Pang was the Colleges Co-ordinator for CUSU International with the daunting task of organizing a network of international students' representatives from the colleges. It was certainly not an easy job because there were quite a number of colleges without an international students' officer. Some colleges actually seemed to resist CUSU International's efforts to encourage establishing a position within the college student union's executive committee.

Some colleges reluctantly established an international students' officer but did not give him/her the status of the college executive officer. For instance, Jesus College, Cambridge, has an international officer but he/she is in a sub-committee dealing with welfare issues. Thus, only the Welfare Officer, who heads the sub-committee, has the executive status and powers within the executive committee of college student government. It is possible to see how a secondary position can weaken the representation of international students in colleges and in the university-wide structure. Any Pang worked hard within the difficult reality to ensure that international students are represented at each college through official channels. I would say that Andy was moderately successful. Not all colleges were fully supportive, but Andy found a good group of colleges with supportive college student union officers with whom he was able to work.

Andy Pang, the College Co-ordinator, worked closely with Mai Yasuhara, the Publicity Officer of CUSU International. Mai sent out weekly newletters – particularly targeting college international students' representatives and ethnic/international student groups. The newsletter contained information of benefit to international students and important information, such as the Visa Renewal Fee.

Mai Yasuhara, CUSU Internatioal Publicity Officer

Andy Pang and Mai Yasuhara were faithful in relaying information to all the colleges in their struggle to get each college involved in issues that concern international students.

It would not be wrong to say, however, that their regular work was helped largely by the aggressive work of Shan-Yee Fok, the Freshers' Officer of CUSU International. Using war imagery, Shan-Yee Fok can be seen as the bomber that first goes and drops a whole load of bombs to flatten the enemy line as much as possible for the ground tanks to move in. Andy Pang and Mai Yasuhara were like the tanks.

In a sense, Shan-Yee had the hardest role in the beginning. The Freshers' week is in

October and she needed to start organizing, planning, getting people together from day one.

Given that the new term for 2003-2004 started in April 22, 2003 for the new CUSU International officers, that did not leave enough time. It is important to note that there is about 8 weeks in a Cambridge University term, so Shan-Yee Fok had 8 weeks before students (including most of the student government officers) left the university for the long summer vacation. Shan-Yee had to do most of the work of the Freshers' fair before leaving Cambridge in June.

Like Anna-Mae Koo, CUSU International Chair (and Mai Yasuhara, the Publicity Officer), Shan-Yee Fok studied law. And like a good law student, Shan-Yee approached her task with ruthless efficiency. Shan-Yee prepared a Freshers' handbook and tried aggressively to get every college involved. Shan-Yee tried to convince every college student union to provide CUSU International Freshers' Guide that she created along with information provided by college student unions. As CUSU International Freshers' guide contained useful, and often necessary, information for international students (such as banking and police registration of foreigners), it supplemented Freshers' guides provided by the university (often, very inadequate on matters pertaining to international students) and college Freshers' guides, often intended for British students.

Although not all the colleges agreed to distribute CUSU International Freshers' Guide to international students entering their college, many colleges did. It was certainly a victory for Shan-Yee Fok and CUSU International as we worked hard to bring about a unity of support for international students.

Some colleges made their own Freshers' guide for international students. One such example is Trinity College, Cambridge, which tends to have a high concentration of international students. Although it would have been nice if they worked with us more integrally, we were happy with the fact that they were proactively working to provide useful information to international students.

2003-2004 can be seen as a transition year for CUSU International. It was then that CUSU International entered Cambridge University student political scene with full force. CUSU International existed for a couple of years, but it was not doing anything really constructive on a lasting level. CUSU International kind of existed as an appendage to CUSU to look like CUSU cared about international students. But with 2003-2004, it was not merely about appearances. It was about making a real difference.

Perhaps, we can't blame CUSU International committees that came before because in many ways, their hands were tied. And there was too much to do, in terms of infrastructure building. Most of the work was from ground zero. We can say that CUSU International committees that came before laid some important building blocks. But it was CUSU International committee of 2003-2004 that really worked hard to build the infrastructure, muscled its way into CUSU and into university structures, and forced the British government to take notice.

I don't doubt that CUSU International won many hearts and did much good for the international student community. However, like all struggles, it would not be inaccurate to say that we made enemies without knowing we did. Not everyone is interested in giving more representation to international students. Not everyone is interested in sharing power with a bunch of people of color. As an American, I understand the scope of the struggle of the Civil Rights movement and its ramifications. After all, was not Martin Luther King, Jr. shot to death?

Thankfully, we were too busy doing work for international students to think about the enemies we were making or the feathers we ruffled. Andrew Pang (Colleges Co-ordinator), Mai Yasuhara (Publicity Officer), and Shan-Yee Fok (Freshers' Officer) led the way in unifying the Cambridge University structure in a way that put the interests of the international student community at the foreground of discussion.

It was, of course, not all work and politics that brought about the unity solution.

CUSU International worked hard to provide social venues for international students to meet each other and for British students to get to know international students in a friendly environment.

In the Michaelmas Term (October 7-December 5, 2003), CUSU International negotiated with the COW at the central area of Cambridge to hold "East Meets West" social nights. The entrance was free in order to make the venue accessible. "East Meets West" social nights were often highly successful. CUSU International provided the DJ and the all kinds of international music that could not be found easily in Cambridge, such as Indian traditional music combined with hip-hop, music from Eastern Europe, music in many different languages, etc. Students could purchase food and drinks from the venue. Although we did not make much profit from the venture, it did not cost us anything to rent the venue. "East Meets West" provided CUSU International with the opportunity to hold a serious and weekly social program on our own with the constructive purpose of unifying international students and British students. As such, it was highly successful and acted to empower international students in the Cambridge University social scene.

Besides casual social programs, we organized more formal events. Andy Pang, the Colleges Co-ordinator of CUSU International, organized the Christmas Dinner on November

27, 2003. It was highly successful with about 65 students attending. We were enthusiastic that Black Students' Campaign officially joined in the festivities.

Christian Kim, CUSU International Academic Officer, puts on a happy face for international students coming to the COW as CUSU International DJ, Tim Coughlan, jams on.

I did my part in trying to organize social programs for international students at Cambridge University. I was entrusted with organizing the biggest formal event of the year: The International Formal Hall.

My focus was to make the program classy, fun, and inexpensive. All international students should be able to come to the fancy shindig without having to worry about the cost.

I was able to work with Ronan Workman, the International Students' Officer at

Churchill College, Cambridge, to organize the International Formal Hall at Churchill College. Thankfully, the price was kept well-below eating out in Cambridge and even cheaper than the price of lunch at Pizza Hut.

Given that the formal dinner is a fancy 4 course meal that is served, it would be impossible to beat the price.

The advert for the event is included below:

CUSU International
http://www.cusu.cam.ac.uk/representation/international

presents

INTERNATIONAL FORMAL HALL

Date: Monday, February 9, 2004 (7 pm)

Place: Churchill College

Special Dance after International Formal

Cost: 6.5 pounds

Confirm your place by sending a check for £6.5 made out to "H. Christian Kim" (write on the back (1) name (2) email (3) college (4) meal option (vegetarian?) to:

H. Christian Kim
CUSU International Formal
Jesus College
Cambridge
CB5 8BL

For more information, contact Christian at International-Academic@cusu.cam.ac.uk

---

The formal hall turned out to be the biggest formal hall ever to be held for international students in the history of Cambridge University. A new record at Cambridge University was set. Over 120 Cambridge University students and their guests attended the festive and chic black-tie event. As the event was historic, the names of the student participants are reproduced here:

CUSU International Formal Hall 2004

(1) Qingyang Yan (Clare College)
(2) A. Meleika Goonerstne (New Hall)
(3) Michelle Butler (Wolfson College)
(4) Boxi Li (Homerton College)
(5) Tiffany Lo (Magdalene College)
(6) Rachel Yu (Trinity College)

CUSU International 2003 - 2004

(7) Gloria Tam (Trinity College)
(8) Elaine Ng (Magdalene)
(9) Daniel Imhof (King's College)
(10) Joerg Gsponer (Robinson College)
(11) Nina Banerjee (Wolfson College)
(12) Maria Ehenbratt (Wolfson College)
(13) Amy Bates (Queens' College)
(14) Bulat Betalgiry (Queens' College)
(15) Christof Roelker (Queens' College)
(16) Dan Choate (Queens' College)
(17) Bin Wu (Queens' College)
(18) guest of Bin Wu (Queens' College)
(19) Qian Li (Queens' College)
(20) Petri Tumola (Queens' College)
(21) Ioulia Timochkina (Queens' College)
(22) Alex Mair (Queens' College)
(23) Milo Prelevic (Queens' College)
(24) Will Bond (Queens' College)
(25) sister of Will Bond (Queens's College)
(26) Bettina Wittneben (Queens' College)
(27) Tracey Pierre (Queens' College)
(28) Gabrielle Robilliard (Wolfson College)
(29) Lauri Personen (Wolfson College)
(30) Guillermo Ramos-Tomas (Jesus College)
(31) Carman Mak (Clare College)
(32) Zara Cheng (Carman Mak's friend)
(33) Ann Shi-Yi Chen (Wolfson College)
(34) Tamir Saeed (Trinity College)
(35) Z. B. J. Strimpel (Jesus College)
(36) Inga Kenter (Trinity Hall)
(37) Marieke Molenkamp (Trinity College)
(38) Karen Haegemans (Corpus Christi College)
(39) Angela Kuhr (Darwin College)
(40) Anna-Mae Koo (Peterhouse)
(41) Dheer Mehta (Peterhouse)
(42) Mai Yasuhara (Wolfson College)
(43) Christian Kim (Jesus College)
(44) Leah Aw (Emmanuel College)
(45) Shan-Yee Fok (Trinity College)
(46) Earl Deng (Fitzwilliam College)

(47) Simon Brennan (Jesus College)
(48) Sue Young (Jesus College)
(49) Sophia Firoz (Lucy Cavendish College)
(50) Michelle Fossey (Lucy Cavendish College)
(51) Nives Mikelic (Hughes Hall)
(52) Aleksandra Gruevska (Darwin College)
(53) Kenneth Wong (Trinity Hall)
(54) Kate Franks (Wolfson College)
(55) Farah Jindani (Wolfson College)
(56) Rhiannen Thomas (Wolfson College)
(57) Sheenah Shah (Newnham College)
(58) Marcus Durst (Christ's College)
(59) Ulrike Schneeberg (Newnham College)
(60) Zahra Abbas (Newnham College)
(61) Chiraag Bains, (King's College)
(62) Rajini Haraksingh (Sidney Sussex College)
(63) Oneil Bhalala (Cauis College)
(64) Tachya Brobbey
(65) Alex Brobbey
(66) Ian Gascoigne (Darwin College)
(67) Gustavo Rocha (Darwin College)
(68) Kate Kenny (Darwin College)
(69) Hannah Rippin (Darwin College)
(70) Andreas Sattler (Darwin College)
(71) Kathleen Corriveau (Darwin College)
(72) guest of Kathleen Carriveau (Darwin College)
(73) Philip Ford (Magdalene College)
(74) guest 1 of Philip Ford (Magdalene College)
(75) guest 2 of Philip Ford (Magdalene College)
(76) Y. P. Samantha Ng (Magdalene College)
(77) Y. N. Lee (Magdalene College)
(78) W. Lala (Magdalene College)
(79) S. P. Ong (Magdalene College)
(80) Q. T. Vuong (Magdalene College)
(81) Angelina Lai (Newnham College)
(82) Alix Bayle (Newnham College)
(83) Jamil Bacha (Wolfson College)
(84) Davina Stevenson (St. John's College)
(85) Eve Woolfson (Newnham College)
(86) Tim Coughlan (Churchill College)

CUSU INTERNATIONAL 2003 - 2004

(87) Giuseppe Di Graziano (Wolfson College)
(88) Shelly Ann Meade (Emmanuel College)
(89) Bryan Coll (Emmanuel College)
(90) Asha Brooks (Emmanuel College)
(91) Antoinette Odoi (Emmanuel College)
(92) Susi Henry (Emmanuel College)
(93) Raghav Kapoor (Pembroke College)
(94) I. Khan (Wolfson College)
(95) Sarah Chin (New Hall)
(96) Charles Kwok (Emmanuel College)
(97) Siau Yin Goh (St. Catharine's College)
(98) Kenneth Wong (Fitzwilliam College)
(99) Wenyi Ding (Queens' College)
(100) Matthew Chiu (Christ's College)
(101) Lisheng Tan (Christi's College)
(102) Bernard Toh (St. Catharine's College)
(103) Timothy Ang (Corpus Christi College)
(104) Ben Sun (Corpus Christi College)
(105) Mark Ho (Girton College)
(106) Adeline Aw (Christ's College)
(107) Shenglong Li (Homerton College)
(108) Chung gee (Trinity Hall)
(109) Eka Wong (Queens' College)
(110) Jean Foo (St. John's College)
(111) Wei-Xian Wang (Caius College)
(112) Melissa Hong (Newnham College)
(113) Paul Tan (Trinity College)
(114) Kah Yong Tan (Christ's College)
(115) Eleanor Fung (Downing College)
(116) Michele Wong (Homerton College)
(117) Heather Felix (Sidney Sussex College)
(118) Jessica Vechakul (St. John's College)
(120) Kathleen Connolly (Trinity Hall)
(121) Stephanie Guo (St. John's College)
(122) Shinny Cho (Newnham College)
(123) guest of Shinny Cho (Newnham College)

CUSU International Formal Hall at Churchill College, Cambridge, was a tremendous success. It looked like a night at Cannes Film Festival with people so well-dressed with much international flare and flavor.

CUSU International Formal Hall, like other social events, was meant to foster a spirit of unity among the international students and also provide opportunities for British students to meet international students.

Unity was, in fact, an overarching theme not only in social programs but also in political and lobbying activities. CUSU International tried to solicit participation in the unity for the benefit of international students – for the long-run common good.

CUSU International officers for 2003-2004 worked very hard, and we accomplished more than we set out to achieve. The history is too short to measure the extent of the impact, but even with such a short passage of time, we cannot deny concrete results that came about from our hard labors.

When we examine Cambridge University structure of today and Cambridge University structure of a couple of years ago, we will notice many structural changes. Some of the key structural changes is due to the fact that we were there and we worked proactively to change things. History cannot deny us our labors and the fruits of our labors.

Of course, there is far more to be done. The officers of CUSU International 2003-2004 hope that the proceeding CUSU Internatinal committees will build on our hard work and advance the interests of international students at Cambridge University and in the United Kingdom.

Section 5: My Articles

CUSU INTERNATIONAL 2003 - 2004

During the course of the 2003-2004 CUSU International term, Earl Deng, the CUSU International Social Officer, maintained our official website with useful information for international students. There was a section on the website for articles reporting on events that CUSU International sponsored and other events of interest to international students. I became a makeshift journalist to report on events of interest to international students. My articles are included here.

"CUSU International Welfare Committee"

CUSU International newly formed the International Welfare Committee to deal with welfare issues pertaining to international students. This committee was formed with the understanding that greater resources must be allocated to examining the situation of international students in the immediate context of Cambridge and in the larger context of the United Kingdom. Current issues being addressed are visa renewal fees and greater access/representation of international students. We are seeking volunteers to work in the committee. If you are interested, please contact Welfare Officer Leah Aw at International-Welfare@cusu.cam.ac.uk

Leah Aw (right) talks with international students

Cambridge University Freshers' Fair 2003

"Freshers' Fair 2003"

CUSU Freshers' Fair held at Kelsey Kerridge on 7-8 October 2003 was highly successful. CUSU International participated actively in order to be of service to international students. Hundreds of students signed up to receive regular emails that can be of use to them. (Weekly emails are sent out to each Cambridge college via the college international reps.) Students from all over the world – from Germany to Russia to China to Australia – showed interest in participating actively in Cambridge life and benefiting from the services of CUSU International. It was at the Freshers' Fair that CUSU International launched the advertisement campaign for the weekly international party night at the COW.

DJ's (Tim Coughlan and Earl Deng) hard at work for "East Meets West" CUSU International nights at the COW

Leah Aw with a volunteer at the Cambridge train station

"Freshers Welcome at the Bus Station"

CUSU International Welfare Officer Leah Aw (Emmanuel College) showed great leadership in organizing welcome of international students at the Bus Station and at the Cambridge Train Station. There were many volunteers mobilized to provide around-the-clock assistance to international students. The welcome program left a lasting, good first impression among international students and made them even happier to be in Cambridge. Such programs will certainly help in advancing diversity in Cambridge and in raising the reputation of Cambridge University even further in the international community.

Earl Deng (Social Officer), Anna Mae Koo (Chair), Veronique Marx, Kris-Stella Trump, Mai Yasuhara (Publicity Officer)

"The Ultimate Cambridge Tour"

CUSU International led tours of Cambridge University on Sunday, 5 October 2003. Several tours started from Café Nero. The tour was designed by H. Christian Kim, the Academic Officer, and helpful Freshers' information provided by Shan Yee Fok, the Freshers' Officer, such as banking information, was incorporated into the tour. This is the first time that such a tour was held for international students by Cambridge's student government, and hopefully it won't be the last. The hour-long tour was meant to be both fun and informative. Participants seemed quite pleased with the tour.

Participants of the tour listen attentively to Anna-Mae Koo, CUSU International Chair, who led a tour

---

"Local Businesses Support CUSU International"

Local businesses have been very supportive of the vision of CUSU International to help international students in Cambridge University. For instance, Mr. Emdadul Haque, the owner of SUBWAY in 40 Mill Road, Cambridge (Tel: 01223-461323), kindly donated three tray full of subway sandwiches for CUSU International Freshers' Squash on 11th October 2003, held at Peterhouse, Cambridge. Also, Lan Hong House in 10 Lensfield Road (Tel: 01223-350420) donated dozens of chicken fried rice packages for the Freshers' Squash. Other sponsors for the Freshers' Squash included WSS Multicard (http://cambridge.wssmulticard.com). We hope that local businesses will continue to support the important work of CUSU International to help international students.

Academic Officer Christian Kim with Mr. Emdadul Haque, the owner of SUBWAY

"Funds for Summer Study Abroad"

There are possibilities to do research abroad during the summer. Being abroad for any length of time can be interesting and beneficial in terms of personal growth. But international experience can be academically and professionally rewarding as well. And you will be happy to know that there are funds available from your college and your faculty/department for such visits. So, you have nothing to lose and everything to gain! It would be advisable to visit a college tutor or a faculty representative to discuss what options there are, and the best time to do so is during the Michaelmas Term. Deadlines for application tend to be in the Michaelmas Term or Lent Term.

"European Food Fair Celebrates European Union"

CUSU International actively supports the work of international students and student societies to share international culture and history in Cambridge. In this regard, we applaud the European Food Fair, sponsored on Friday, 7 November 2003, by the European Union Society, the Belarusian Society, the Central European Society, the German Society, the

Hellenic Society, the Russian Society, and the Ukranian Society.

The event was well-organized under the leadership of Helene Reiter of St. Catharine's College, the Ents Officer of the European Union Society. Many visitors were greeted personally by Helene or by equally friendly Eduardo Tamraz of King's College, the Treasurer of the European Union Society.

One of many happy faces at the European Food Fair

The School of Pythagoras at St. John's College, where the food fair was held, was filled with excited people, ready to try new cuisine. Philip Ford, the president of the International Society, gave credit to the societies for their wonderful work: "You have to make a real effort to achieve anything in Cambridge." And it was obvious that a lot of work and care have been put into organizing the event. The event drew praises from attendees. Dominic Wulffen, a second year SPS concentrator from Christ's College, exclaimed: "Great variety of stuff here!" Equally enthusiastic was Carter Liang, a second year Mathematics concentrator from Girton College, who admitted that he was glad to be there "to try something new."

Volunteers from societies participating were equally enthusiastic about the event. Andrew Ivanchenko, a Ph.D. student in English at Trinity College, who is a Social Officer for the Ukranian Society, enthused that it was good "to share our culture – in this case, food culture." Looking around the room full of people, Ivanchenko commented: "This is the kind of integration that we are interested in."

Looking around the room, one could see participants actively integrating dishes from different countries. Starters included Belarusian Borsch from the Belarusian Society and Greek salad from the Hellenic Society. Main courses included dark German bread from the German Society and cured fish Baltic style from the Central European Society. Bliny (Russian pancakes) from the Russian Society satiated hungry souls both as an appetizer and a main course dish. Syrnyk (cheesecake with raisins and candied peel) from the Ukranian

Society served as a nice finale to the whole culinary experience.

The European Food Fair was more than about food items from different countries. It was an expression of hope and dreams for a better world, a more harmonious society. Ivanchenko explained that even though Ukraine was not officially a part of the European Union, "we are geographically in Europe, so we are here." When asked if Ukraine should be a part of the European Union, Ivanchenko said with thoughtful hope in his eyes: "Of course, we should be. And we will be at some point."

Eduardo Tamraz, the Treasurer of the European Union Society at Cambridge University, welcomes visitors

"Friendship Game Between Malaysians and Koreans"

There are many international and ethnic societies in Cambridge, and many students benefit from involvement in these societies. It is good to see the societies taking initiative and trying to develop friendships with members from different societies. Sometimes various societies have friendly competitions in sports with each other. Last Saturday (15 November 2003), the Cambridge University Korean Society (CUKS) and the Cambridge University Malaysian Society (CUMaS) played a friendly football match at Sidney Sussex College Sports Grounds. H. Christian Kim, the Academic Officer of CUSU International (also, the president of the Cambridge University Korean Society from 2002-2003) was there to cover the match and interview students. Video clips of interviews and the game can be seen at the following link: http://cuks_cumas.tripod.com

If you are interested in joining one of the societies in Cambridge, please visit this Cambridge University website for societies: http://www.cam.ac.uk/societies

If you have any general questions, please feel free to contact one of the executive committee members of CUSU International, which exists to help international students and encourage greater understanding and acceptance of them in Cambridge.

Professor Jane Webster gave an academic paper on her new book, Ingesting Jesus: Eating and Drinking in the Gospel of John, at the same Society of Biblical Literature conference section as Christian Kim's

"Emory University and International Studies Opportunity in the USA"

I went to the Society of Biblical Literature Annual Meeting (22-25 November 2003) in Atlanta, Georgia, USA, to deliver an academic paper on the Gospel of John, and I had the pleasure of visiting Emory University, an academic institution of higher education that is under the auspices of the United Methodist Church (Duke University, Boston University, Northwestern University are among other elite universities belonging to the United Methodist Church). I wanted to do something for Cambridge University students, so I looked for programs which some Cambridge students might be interested in. I came across one that could be of interest particularly to law and theology students, although students in other faculties can certainly participate in it.

Emory University's Center for Interdisciplinary Study in Religion, which is housed in the law faculty of Emory University, offers many opportunities for students and scholars alike who are interested in harnessing the benefits of a legal education and theological training to think about global and domestic issues and offer practical solutions. There are possibilities for independent scholars to conduct research and for students to pursue academic study in a joint degree program.

A Cambridge University graduate can apply to pursue a J.D.-M.Div. degree for instance. Students holding any first degree can apply to this joint program. The Juris Doctor degree is a professional law degree that takes 3 years. The Master of Divinity degree is a degree for ordained ministry (but you can choose not to be ordained after the program), which normally takes 3 years. The combined program offers you the opportunity to receive the two degrees in a relatively shorter time. More importantly, you will have the opportunities to explore issues that are relevant to today using the best minds that the two faculties have to offer. This joint degree is practical as well. You can find positions in service organizations, non-government organizations, and government jobs, which require understanding of world religions, more easily with this joint degree.

I interviewed Ms. Eliza Ellison, the Director of Projects and Research, at the Center for Interdisciplinary Study of Religion at Emory University. Ms. Ellison noted that since the founding of the program in 1982 by Dr. Frank Alexander, who completed his J.D. and M.T.S. (Master of Theological Studies) degrees at Harvard University, the center has engaged in several serious research projects: (1) Christianity and Democracy in the Global Context; (2) Religion and Human Rights; and (3) Proselytism. Each project produced at least a volume of serious academic articles written by participants. Students benefited from the scholars (both Emory faculty and visiting faculty) in residence.

The Center had scholars from Germany and from Oxford, but so far none has come from Cambridge. In fact, it was not just Cambridge scholars, but Cambridge student presence seems to be missing as well. I asked Ms. Ellison if she had met any Cambridge University students, and she said, "No." Ms. Ellison has been in Emory since 1987.

I asked Ms. Ellison if she would be interested in seeing Cambridge scholars and students come to the center, and she expressed her positive answer and said that Cambridge

University symbolizes "prestige, excellence, and intellectuals."

I was surprised that Ms. Ellison had not seen any Cambridge University students, so I took to the streets of Emory University to see how pervasive her experience was. Aram Yang, an Asian American 4th year English major, said that she had not met any Cambridge students either. This seems to be the general experience of many Emory students. Brian Connelly, 4th year psychology major, and Mary Sockolov, a 2nd year business major who intends on studying medicine after her first degree, and Katie Hale, a 2nd year double major in English and Psychology, all admitted that they had not met any Cambridge students.

Although Emory University students have not met any Cambridge students, they all had a positive perception of Cambridge. Mary Sockolov, who left her home in California to study at the academically respected Emory University, exclaimed that Cambridge University is a "prestigious school." Ms. Sockolov said that she would consider studying in Cambridge University in her 4th year. Katie Hale, a very friendly student from Ohio, said that she will definitely look into spending her 3rd year in Cambridge. Aram Yang, who has a friend who participated in the MIT-Cambridge exchange program, said that she would actually consider pursuing her Ph.D. studies in Cambridge.

Mary Sockolov praises Cambridge University

Rasheedah Pickett, a 3rd year psychology major from Georgia, expressed similar praise for Cambridge University as an academically respected university. She, however, noted that prestigious universities, like Cambridge and Emory, can do great things in terms of social responsibility. Ms. Pickett is the president of Emory Read, a program started by Emory University students 7 years ago to tutor inner-city, poor children of Atlanta in reading. Ms. Pickett said: "It is important for them to see what the future is because many times they don't get out. It is important for them to see what is out there for them."

Rasheedah Pickett is concerned with access issues

The impression that I was left with after my visit to Emory University is that it is a socially conscientious university. There are university sanctioned academic programs that indicate a sense of social responsibility, and there are student initiated programs that try to meet the needs of those in need. Cambridge University graduates can give as much as receive. Cambridge students can bring their excellent academic training to add to the discourse on issues relating to law, theology, and society, for instance, in the context of the Center for Interdisciplinary Study of Religion. And Emory University has a lot to teach as one of the leading institutions in the United States dealing with issues on poverty and the inner city.

It would be wonderful to see a Cambridge graduate pursuing a J.D.-M.Div. degree and participating in Emory Read.

For more information about Emory University, visit their website at http://www.emory.edu

"CUSU International Celebrates Christmas"

CUSU International sponsored International Christmas Dinner at Sidney Sussex College on Thursday, 27 November 2003 – about a week before the end of Michaelmas Term, 2003. Black Students' Campaign threw their official support of CUSU International's efforts to provide a classy celebration of international students in Cambridge.

Andy Pang, Colleges Co-ordinator of CUSU International, was the mastermind behind the organization of the event, taking painstaking attention to detail down to the last bottle of wine. About 65 students paid 15 pounds each to participate in this classy affair.

CUSU International Chair Anna Mae Koo takes a photo with her fans at the CUSU International Christmas Dinner

Students from many different countries, socio-economic backgrounds, and ethnic groups participated in a spirit of friendship and fellowship. Soon, it became obvious that everyone was enjoying themselves and making new friends.

After the Christmas Dinner, the dinner participants headed to Coco's and were given first-class treatment with free VIP passes (no waiting in line). Many from the dinner were seen dancing away even at 1:30 AM.

CUSU International is planning other such fun events in the future, so please check back regularly for announcements.

"The Meeting of Two Legal Worlds: France and England Shake Hands"

There is a reason why Cambridge University is a leading academic institution in the world. One of the important reasons is the presence of quality international students who add not only to cultural diversity but also to Cambridge's academic curriculum. Like the Papacy in twelfth century Medieval Europe, which wisely and quickly institutionalized itinerant monastic movements of St. Francis ant St. Dominic which enriched the Christian community and its intellectual pursuits, many Cambridge faculties are institutionalizing foreign student involvement in Cambridge.

The Double-Maitrise program in the Faculty of Law is one such enlightened endeavor. The law studies program, which started in October 1999, allows ten students from Cambridge University and ten students from the University of Paris II, Assas, to receive both British and French law qualifications in four years. Twenty students spend their first two years in Cambridge and last two years in Paris. The strength of the program is that at the end of the four years, the graduates will have two law degrees from different countries and they will be able to work either in England or France. Implications for International Law are obvious.

Law students from France take a break from their hard-studying at Cambridge University

Double-Maitrise is an elite program and very difficult to get into. Marie Gaschignard of Emmanuel College who is in the second year of the program at Cambridge said that Paris II, Assas, takes particular attention to the English language abilities of French students who are interested in the program since French students will have to take law courses alongside English students at Cambridge. Miss Gaschignard said, "You have to take a written exam like the Cambridge Advanced so that they can see how good your English is. If it is good, then they will give you an interview."

Of course, French students who are here in Cambridge are the elite of their bunch and not just in their English language skills. Florian Quintard of Trinity College, who is also from Paris, showed off his intellectual acquisition in the area of law. Mr. Quintard enthusiastically commented that he was fascinated by the flexibility of English law and its application. He explained, "In France, law is codified and rules are clear. There is seldom any ambiguity as in England. Judges in France merely apply the law, but it seems judges have more power in England."

Linda Ikhlef of Robinson College commented that the key difference is due to the nature of Constitutional Law in the two countries. With the debate about the Constitution of the European Union raging at the moment, perhaps some of the Double-Maitrise students will play an important role in the future of European Constitutional Law.

It was not only the intellectual contribution of Cambridge academics that captured the hearts of the French students studying away from their home. Miss Gaschignard said, "I enjoy the Cambridge formal hall and English traditions in Cambridge." Mr. Quintard agreed that he is very happy to be participating in the program in the United Kingdom. As much as she was enjoying her time in Cambridge, Miss Ikhlef confessed, "I miss French food." Mais oui, elle est francaise!

Information about the Double-Maitrise program can be obtained through the Faculty of Law (http://www.law.cam.ac.uk/courses/) in Cambridge and also through the University of Paris II, Assas (http://www.u-paris2.fr). And the Double-Maitrise Association will be launching their own website soon at http://www.DoubleMatrise.com.

"Cambridge Joins Warwick in the Spirit of Oneness"

12 noon marked the departure from Queens Road of smiling Cambridge University students and their guests.

In the spirit of supporting tolerance toward different cultures and ideas, CUSU International created an opportunity for Cambridge University students to participate in the One World Week in Warwick for a day and subsidized the trip. Warwick University's One World Week is the biggest of its kind, and the grand finale event, The One World Party, on Saturday, 24 January, 2004, did not disappoint.

Dheer Mehta (Secretary), Andy Pang (Colleges Co-Ordinator), Anna-Mae Koo (Chair), Christian Kim (Academic Officer), and Shan-Yee Fok (Freshers' Officer) are enthusiastic about One World Week

There were over 3,000 people in attendance, and more than enough food for every person in attendance. 22 food stalls from cuisines ranging from Bahai to Israeli provided generous portions for those hungry for different cultural experiences and eager for culinary satisfaction.

My culinary journey started at the enticing Sri Lanka food stall, followed by a pleasant stop at the Baobab (African Societies) food stop, and concluded in the wonders of the African/Caribbean food stall. Friendly faces gave generous portions in the spirit of celebration, and I noticed that my face was not the only one smiling with enjoyment. Eager faces looked this way and that for the next fix, and we looked at each other, acknowledging the powerful pull in collective understanding.

There was so much wonderful food to try that as dinner time came to a close, many were still trying to get a bit more of the culinary ecstasy. Throwing all sense of pride to the wind, I found myself standing in front of the Nordic food stall, trying to persuade a German guy in Lederhosen not to close the stall and make a fresh waffle desert. Although my well reasoned arguments seemed to fall on his seemingly deaf ears, two pouting German blonde ladies standing next to me seemed to open his eyes and heart to our need. Three of us took eager turns from the new batch. It was a glorious food party.

I asked the German student next to me what she thought about the event. Miss Kristin Muehle, an Eramus student from Zitau University in Germany studying Translation/Interpretation praised the celebration of diversity and pointed out that such culturally diverse event would not be possible without the presence of international students.

And without international students, the diversity of cultural performances would not have been possible either. After dinner, the guests were treated to a cultural extravaganza with 26 performances, ranging from latest Bollywood top charts to the grand finale of seductive Arabic dance. One after next, cultureally diverse performances showed the greatness that exists in the global community and indicated the unlimited potential of cultural sharing.

It was obvious that a lot of effort went into this glorious celebration of diversity.

Miss Cynthia Mbaru, a 3rd year Mathematics and Economics major working with Baobab (African Society) explained that preparations started in the morning with food preparation. Food preparation was followed by final dance practices in the afternoon. In the evening, the intelligent and beautiful Miss Mbaru along with her friends from Baobab gave us an opportunity at tasting her paradise, first with food and then with the wonderfully choreographed African dance.

It was clear that Miss Mbaru thought all the hard effort very worthwhile. When asked what she thought was the best thing about the One World Week, she said without hesitation, "It is a good opportunity for people who are not a part of UK to show what they are about. We can dispel negative stereotypes and show the diversity of Africa."

Mr. Chen, a member of the Hong Kong Society and a 2nd year studying electronic engineering, showed his enthusiasm for the One World Week from another angle. Mr. Chen said that the best thing about the event promoting tolerance was the opportunity for British students to learn about foreign cultures and students. He was glad that this event drew many home students.

In the midst of joyful celebration of diversity at Warwick University, there was a sad note that seemed to mar the otherwise a perfect event. Foreign students seemed concerned about the new Visa Renewal Fee introduced in 1st August 2003, that charges up to 250 pounds for each student visa renewal. It used to be free to renew student visas.

Mr. Chen, who left Hong Kong to study in the UK since his GCSE, shared his troubles. Although he produced a letter from the University of Warwick stating that he was a student at the University until 2006, his visa was renewed for only one year by the Home Office. He paid 155 pounds for visa renewal and will have to pay anywhere from 155-250 pounds for visa renewal again in a year's time.

But for this day, international students tried to push aside their troubles and unselfishly shared the wonders of their cultures.

It was this joy that we took back with us to Cambridge as we drove away from Warwick at 12 midnight.

About the Author

Christian Kim is a Ph.D. candidate in Hebrew, Jewish, and Early Christian Studies at the University of Cambridge in Great Britain. He was elected as the Academic Officer of CUSU International by Cambridge University students for the first time to serve the 2002-2003 term. Christian Kim was re-elected as the Academic Officer of CUSU International for the 2003-2004 term. During that time, Christian Kim has been very active in bringing issues facing international students to the foreground of Cambridge University discussions. Christian Kim continues to think seriously about issues facing international students and the people of color. Christian Kim has also written an introductory book on the Korean community in the United States of America, entitled, *Korean-American Experience in the United States: Initial Thoughts*.

www.ingramcontent.com/pod-product-compliance
Lightning Source LLC
LaVergne TN
LVHW041627070426
835507LV00008B/487